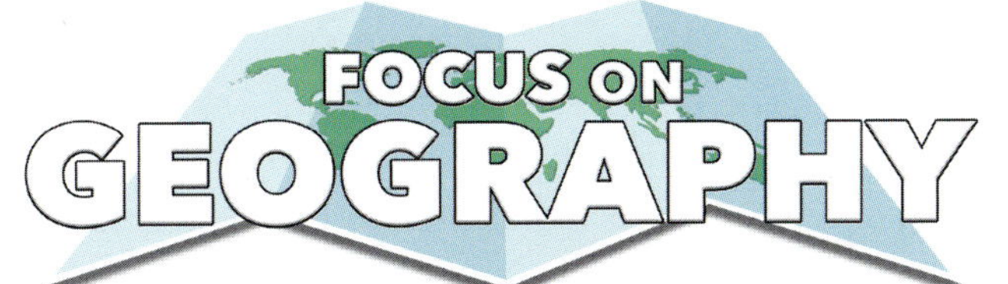

Focus on Chile

Linda Barghoorn

A Crabtree Forest Book

Crabtree Publishing
crabtreebooks.com

Author: Linda Barghoorn

Series research and development:
Janine Deschenes

Editorial director: Kathy Middleton

Editor: Crystal Sikkens

Proofreader: Melissa Boyce

Design: Tammy McGarr

Print and production coordinator:
Katherine Berti

IMAGE CREDITS

Alamy: Galaxiid p 44 (bottom)

Goldman Environmental Prize: p 45 all images

iStock: Grafissimo, p 17 (top); Global_Pics p 21 (top), p 23 (bottom); Dr John A Horsfall, p 40 (bottom)

NASA: p 41

Shutterstock: Michele Rinaldi, front cover (top left); Pablo Rogat, title page, p 35 (top); Alexandre Laprise, p 5 (bottom left); Matyas Rehak, p 8 (middle); Felipe Fredes Fernandez, p 12 (top); Ksenia Ragozina, p 12 (middle); Joao Kermadec, p 14 (top left); Claudine Van Massenhove, p 14 (right); Gubin Yury, p 21 (bottom); Locomotive74, p 22 (bottom); Art Konovalov, p 23 (top), p 26 (top); DFLC Prints, p 26 (bottom); reisegraf.ch, p 27 (top); Felix Malte Dorn, p 28 (top); abriendomundo, p 31 (top); gonzagon, p 31 (middle); William Cushman, p 31 (bottom); Anton_Ivanov, p 32; Mauricio Quevedo, p 37; abriendomundo, p 39 (top)

Wikimedia Commons: Public Domain p 4 (inset), p 19, p 33 (top); p 20 (bottom), p 35 (bottom); Creative Commons, p 10 (bottom), p 15 (top), p 18 (left), p 29 (top), p 33 (botton), p 36 (top), p 36 (bottom), p 43 (bottom)

Crabtree Publishing

crabtreebooks.com 800-387-7650
Copyright © 2023 Crabtree Publishing

All rights reserved. No part of this publication may be reproduced, stored in a retrieval system or be transmitted in any form or by any means, electronic, mechanical, photocopying, recording, or otherwise, without the prior written permission of Crabtree Publishing Company.
In Canada: We acknowledge the financial support of the Government of Canada through the Canada Book Fund for our publishing activities.

Hardcover 978-1-0398-0642-9
Paperback 978-1-0398-0668-9
Ebook (pdf) 978-1-0398-0694-8
Epub 978-1-0398-0721-1

Published in Canada
Crabtree Publishing
616 Welland Avenue
St. Catharines, Ontario
L2M 5V6

Published in the United States
Crabtree Publishing
347 Fifth Avenue
Suite 1402-145
New York, New York, 10016

Library and Archives Canada Cataloguing in Publication
Available at Library and Archives Canada

Library of Congress Cataloging-in-Publication Data
Available at the Library of Congress

Printed in the U.S.A./012023/CG20220815

Contents

INTRODUCTION 4

CHAPTER 1
The Land 8

CHAPTER 2
Becoming Chile 16

CHAPTER 3
Life Today 24

CHAPTER 4
A Vibrant Country 32

CHAPTER 5
Looking to the Future 40

Glossary 46

Learning More 47

Index 48

About the Author 48

Introduction

Llamas and alpacas are **domesticated** animals found in the Altiplano. The Aymara use them for their wool and meat.

The Aymara began to settle in the Altiplano region around 900 years ago.

Snapshot of Life in the Altiplano

The Altiplano region of northern Chile boasts landscapes that are both harsh and beautiful. The **steppe** high in the Andes mountain range is made up of **arid** deserts, wide grasslands, salt flats, and **fertile** valleys. The climate can be harsh, and the soil is sometimes poor. Despite this, it is home to some of the earliest inhabitants of South America.

For hundreds of years, the Aymara have lived in small villages in these highlands. They cut **terraces** into the steep grassy slopes to plant crops. The **coarse** mountain grasses provide plentiful food for their sheep, alpaca, and llama herds. These animals are well-suited to the cold, dry climate of the Altiplano. The people plant staple crops like potato, maize (or corn), and quinoa. They also grow oca and ullucu—root vegetables that are **native** to this region. The cold climate makes it possible to preserve potatoes outdoors where they are dried and pounded into small pieces known as *chuño*. It is a key ingredient in *chairo*—a traditional dish made of potatoes, onions, carrots, corn, meat, and coriander.

Aymara homes are built from materials found in the surrounding environment.

Aymara Traditions

A traditional Aymara home is a one-room, **adobe**-style house. The walls are made of mud and stone, while the thatched roof is made of wild grass. Extended families live together in a community known as an *ayllu*, where everyone helps one another—building houses, raising children, and harvesting crops. Families are often quite large, with up to seven or eight children.

The Aymara believe that spirits share their mountain home. Pachamama—the Earth Goddess—is the most important. She has the power to ensure good crops, the key to the tribe's survival. Traditional dances celebrate harvests and other important events. Often, they include brightly colored masks and costumes. Music is played on drums, flutes, and the *pututu*. Weaving is a centuries-old practice that uses the thick, lush wool of alpacas and llamas to make a variety of clothes and blankets to keep the people warm during the long, cold, winter months.

A *pututu* is a trumpet-like instrument carved out of a cow horn.

The Aymara have a complex system of dyeing and often include a variety of colors in their weaving.

Introducing Chile

Chile is an extremely long, narrow country, which spans more than half of the length of the South American continent and ends at its southernmost tip. Its name is thought to have come from an **Indigenous** word, meaning "where the land ends." The Pacific coastline is almost 4,000 miles (6,437 km) long. The towering Andes Mountains dominate the landscape. They create a huge barrier which separates Chile from neighboring Argentina, Bolivia, and Peru.

Because of its length from north to south, Chile experiences a wide range of landscapes and climates. A **fault line** located on the Pacific Ocean floor near the coast has caused violent earthquakes and destructive tsunamis which threaten coastal settlements. Chile's southernmost tip is only 400 miles (644 km) from Antarctica. It endures some of the harshest weather on Earth, making it a difficult place to live.

Santiago, established by the Spanish in 1541, is Chile's capital city. It is also the country's largest city, with a population of more than 6.5 million people.

Mestizo Identity

Spanish **colonization** began in the 1500s, followed by migration from other parts of Europe. Europeans mixed with the local Indigenous peoples to create a **mestizo** culture that dominates much of modern Chile.

The country's location, rugged landscapes, and challenging climates have served to isolate Chile and its people from its neighbors and the rest of the world. This has helped create a unique Chilean national identity.

Rights of Indigenous Peoples

Of the approximately 2 million Indigenous peoples in Chile today, the Mapuche tribe is the largest. Other tribes include the Aymara, Diaguita, and Quechua peoples. Despite some improvements for the rights of Indigenous peoples, Chile remains the only country in Latin America that does not officially recognize its Indigenous peoples in its **constitution**. As a result, Chile's Indigenous peoples are denied their full rights as Chilean citizens. This has caused difficult issues around land ownership and use of Chile's natural resources.

AT A GLANCE

- **OFFICIAL NAME:** Republic of Chile
- **NATIONAL CAPITAL:** Santiago
- **POPULATION:** 19,412,855
- **OFFICIAL LANGUAGES:** Spanish
- **LAND AREA:** 291,932 square miles (756,100 sq. km)

CHAPTER 1

The Land

Physical Features

Most of Chile's landforms run the length of the country from north to south. The snow-capped Andes Mountains create a barrier that has restricted human migration and settlement from the interior of the continent. Along the Pacific coast, several important cities—like Iquique, Arica, and Valparaiso—have developed as **seaports**. They have provided Chile with important access to countries around the world to which it **exports** its agricultural products and mineral resources.

Rivers running through central Chile deposited silt, sand, and clay over thousands of years to create rich soils in the **temperate** Central Valley. This creates a thriving agricultural area that supports much of Chile's population and economy. The capital city of Santiago has prospered here. Most of Chile's rivers are too rough to be navigated safely or settled alongside. But they provide important hydroelectricity to the country. During the spring, melting snow and **runoff** support **irrigation** for the country's crops.

The Serrano River is in southern Chile. It is part of Torres del Paine National Park.

Valparaiso is an important port that exports mainly copper, wine, and fresh fruit.

By 2024, it is estimated that 45–48 percent of Chile's electricity generation will come from hydropower.

Climate and Weather

Chile's mountain ranges and the Pacific Ocean currents have a huge influence on its climate. The Andes act like an enormous wall that blocks moisture from the east. The Humboldt Current brings cold water from the South Pacific northward along Chile's coast, cooling its temperate coastal climates. The South Pacific High is a system of **anticyclone** winds that create arid conditions on Chile's northern coast. It combines with the Humboldt to establish the conditions that have created the Atacama coastal desert.

Once a water-rich area, the Atacama Desert is now the oldest, driest desert on Earth. It is rich in mineral deposits such as copper, gold, silver, and lithium. These have been important to Chile's economy in recent centuries. But its extreme climate has severely restricted human settlement. In contrast to the northern desert, Chile's southern region has a **subantarctic** climate that is cold, wet, and extremely windy. Like the Atacama Desert, it is largely **inhospitable**.

Large flocks of flamingos are most commonly seen in the Atacama from December to February.

The huemul is a member of the deer family that lives in the southern Andes. It is represented on Chile's coat of arms. It was once widespread, but is now the most endangered deer in South America.

Wildlife

Animal habitats and migrations across Chile are shaped by its ocean coastline, mountain steppes, and northern desert. Thanks to its diverse geography and climate, Chile has one of the most varied bird populations on Earth. The salt flats of the northern Atacama Desert host enormous flocks of flamingos that feast on the lakes' algae and brine shrimps. The carancha—a large bird of prey in the Andes—frequently attacks lambs on livestock ranches that have sprung up in the region. King penguins inhabit the subantarctic regions in the extreme south.

Llamas, alpacas, and vicuñas have thrived on the grasses of the high mountain **plateaus**. For centuries, they have been tended by Indigenous peoples who have used their soft, high-quality wool to perfect the art of weaving. With its long coastline, fishing has long been a staple of Chile's coastal Indigenous populations. Today it is also an important export industry.

Plant Life

The vegetation of the northern Atacama Desert has adapted to the lack of rain and the high salt content of its soils, while coastal fogs support many cacti and shrubs. The semi-arid Norte Chico region marks the transition from desert to the Matorral shrubland forests of native espino and algarrobo hardwoods.

The common ice plant get its water from fog.

The temperate region of central Chile features grasslands and fertile valleys that support the country's thriving agricultural and livestock production. Much of Chile's human settlement has grown around these industries. More than two-thirds of Chile's entire population is based here. But **urbanization** and over-grazing by livestock pose real threats to the environment.

In the high mountain steppes, **hardy** species of grasses—such as ichu—support the Indigenous peoples and their livestock herds. Hardwood forests of the western Andes feature trees like the roble and coigue. Increasingly these forests are being destroyed to make way for modern tree **plantations**, crops, grazing lands, and human settlement.

Hardwood trees were used by the Mapuche tribe to carve canoes. They were also used as firewood for heating and cooking.

Chuquicamata began to convert to an underground mine in 2019 in order to access the remaining copper ore underground.

A Mineral-Rich Country

Chile's mineral resources have played an important role in the country's development since Indigenous peoples first discovered deposits of copper, silver, gold, and iron centuries ago. The Atacama Desert and Norte Chico and Norte Grande regions hold much of Chile's mineral wealth.

The Atacama Desert **oasis** at Copiapo had been farmed since the time of the **Incan civilization**. But the discovery of gold and silver in the 1800s transformed it into one of Chile's key mining centers. Small-scale mining of copper was originally done by individuals known as *pirquineros*, who worked the mines in north-central Chile. Funding from the United States in the 1900s helped Chile expand its operations. Today it is the world's largest copper exporter. Chuquicamata began large-scale mining operations in the early 1900s. Since then it has become one of the world's largest open-pit mines. It is now undergoing a transition to become the largest and most advanced underground mine in the world.

The coastal city of Antofagasta developed as a key export center for copper to markets around the world.

In open-pit mines such as Chuquicamata, miners extract minerals from a pit dug into the ground's surface.

Closer Look

Chile's White Gold

In the 1800s, **nitrate**-based **fertilizers** were developed to improve crops and increase food production to meet the needs of rapidly growing populations. Potassium nitrate—also known as saltpeter—was a key ingredient in these fertilizers. Deposits of this mineral were found in Chile's northern regions. Despite being one of the most uninhabitable places on Earth, towns like Humberstone and Santa Laura were quickly established there. Workers arrived from across the continent, attracted by promises of wealth and prosperity. Potassium nitrate was so highly prized it was nicknamed Chile's "white gold." Peru and Bolivia controlled the Atacama's mineral resources until Chile went to war with them in 1879. When it won, Chile took over the region and its mining activities. At its peak, it controlled 80 percent of the world's production. But demand dropped in the 1930s when scientists developed a human-made version of potassium nitrate. Chile's economy collapsed and the mining towns built around this industry were abandoned. In 2005, they were designated **UNESCO World Heritage sites**, drawing tourists to these deserted **ghost towns**.

A processing plant in Santa Laura is one of many buildings left abandoned after demand for potassium nitrate dropped.

Agriculture

Chile's mountainous terrain means that only about 3 percent of Chile's land is **arable**. The majority of this farming takes place in the temperate Central Valley, where the climate and soil are most suited to growing crops. Grapes, wheat, potatoes, corn, apples, beans, and rice are important crops grown in this region. Small family subsistence farms were common in earlier Indigenous populations who grew just enough fruits and vegetables to feed their families. When Spanish colonizers arrived, they quickly seized control of much of the arable land.

The southern Patagonian steppe was farmed by Indigenous peoples for thousands of years. The region's grasslands were highly suited to growing grain. In the 1800s, large areas of land were offered to attract European settlers. Sheep were introduced from other areas of the continent. Estancias—large sheep ranches—were established under the ownership of private, wealthy families. Since then, Patagonia has grown into one of the world's most important sheep-farming regions, producing both wool and meat.

Many fruits and vegetables grown in the Central Valley are loaded on trucks and brought to wholesale markets.

Potatoes are an important crop in Chile. More than 99 percent of the potato varieties grown around the world originated in Chile.

Chile produces about 24 million pounds (10.9 million kg) of wool a year.

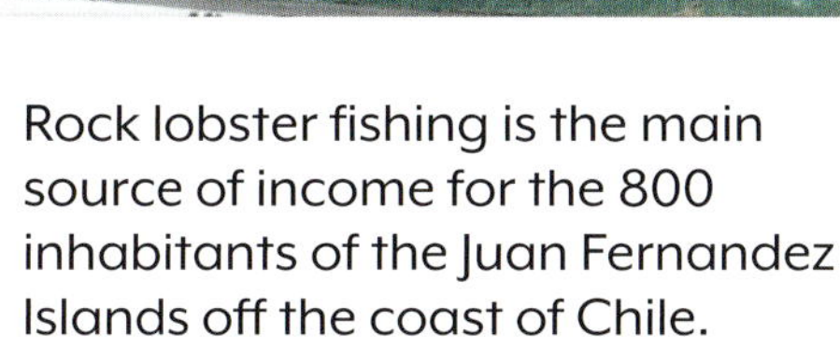

Rock lobster fishing is the main source of income for the 800 inhabitants of the Juan Fernandez Islands off the coast of Chile.

Forestry and Fishing

Southern Chile boasts one of the world's last remaining large rain forests, dominated by coihue and roble trees. Subantarctic boreal forests feature regions of coihue and lenga trees. During colonization, large areas of forest were cleared for agriculture and livestock farms. Since then, illegal logging and expanded human settlement have continued the destruction of Chile's forests. Many large-scale plantations that grow pine and eucalyptus wood for foreign markets have been established on Chile's old-growth forest lands.

Chile's coastal waters have long been an important source of food for Indigenous fishers. Its long coastline spans several climate zones and hosts an abundant and diverse population of seafood, including sardines, anchovies, prawns, shrimp, mackerel, hake, and many others. This has allowed Chile to become one of the world's key seafood exporters. Important fishing ports include Puerto Montt and San Vicente-Talcahuano.

The pine and eucalyptus plantations have helped Chile become an important supplier of wood and paper products. The country mainly exports chips, lumber, and logs to oversea markets.

CHAPTER 2

Becoming Chile

Early Inhabitants

Although little is known about Chile's earliest inhabitants, it is believed that Indigenous peoples migrated there around 20,000–40,000 years ago. Arriving on the Pacific coast, they moved inland to settle the region's fertile valleys and grasslands. From these original settlers, a number of Indigenous regional cultures developed. Most were made up of small tribes scattered across large areas.

Peoples in the North

At one time, the Atacama region was more humid and hospitable to human settlement, attracting **nomadic** groups of hunters and gatherers. Northern Indigenous groups, such as the Aymara people, were influenced by pre-Incan tribes. They developed a range of rich handicrafts, including pottery, textiles, and metalwork. Tribes cultivated simple crops and herded native animals such as the llama.

The Aymara are skilled weavers and spinners who make textiles out of fine yarns made from llama, alpaca, and vicuña wool.

Inhospitable South

The Patagonian culture consisted of largely nomadic tribes that roamed the southern regions of Chile. Their name is derived from the Spanish word *patagon*—or large foot—a possible reference to the size of their feet. Harsh weather and rugged terrain made it difficult for these tribes to settle the region. Most continued to live as hunters or fishers who spent much of their time on the water, traveling in canoes in search of food. The inhospitable conditions of this region have caused it to remain one of the least-developed areas in modern Chile.

The Araucanians

The Araucanian culture makes up the largest Indigenous group in Chile today, and includes the Picunche and Mapuche peoples. They settled in the grasslands and fertile valleys of Chile's south-central region—first as hunters and gatherers, then as farmers. They grew subsistence crops, including corn, beans, squash, and potatoes. But their true wealth was measured by the size of their llama herds, which they used as pack animals and for their thick, warm wool. They lived in tightly knit family groups and participated in both trade and warfare with other Indigenous groups.

Mapuche babies were often carried on their mother's back in a wooden frame cushioned with wool.

Llamas are still used as pack animals and sources of wool and meat.

The Mapuche used large wooden carvings showing human features to mark the grave of a deceased person.

Inca Invaders

The powerful Incan empire spanned a large part of the Andean region of South America. It was famous for its finely crafted gold and silver metalwork and for its woolen textiles. During the 15th century, the Incans conquered a number of local tribes to expand their control over the region's mineral deposits. But they met fierce resistance by the Mapuche people and were defeated by them at the Maule River battle. This river became the boundary between the Incan Empire and Mapuche lands until the arrival of Spanish explorers.

Spanish Conquistadors

In the 16th century, Spanish **conquistadors** landed in Chile in search of an *otro* Peru—another Peru—and its rich mineral resources. Finding neither, the Spanish **colony** grew slowly until they recognized the enormous potential of the Central Valley's fertile land and warmer climate. They took control of much of this land and established a system of large agricultural estates—or haciendas—where they raised livestock and cultivated crops. As they did so, they **displaced** Indigenous peoples from their land. Indigenous farmers were forced to relocate to less fertile areas on which to farm, or to work on the haciendas as poorly paid labor.

The Mapuche territory was south of the Maule River.

Closer Look

The series of conflicts between the Araucanians, including the Mapuches, and the Spanish is known as the Arauco War. The conflicts lasted centuries, from the 1500s to the 1800s.

Indigenous Resistance

More than half a million Mapuche tribespeople lived in the Central Valley where they had made their livelihoods as farmers and fishers for centuries. They were not willing to submit easily to the Spanish colonizers' attempts to steal their land. Instead, they organized villagers to fight the Spanish and formed a ferocious resistance. They learned how to ride the horses the Spanish had brought to Chile and used them to attack the invaders.

For more than three centuries the Mapuche fought the Spanish to keep control of their lands and their way of life. But fighting, disease, and government policies have **marginalized** the Mapuche people. After their defeat, they were forced to sign **treaties** with the Chilean government and settle on **reservations** to the south. While they remain the largest of Chile's Indigenous tribes, they no longer control the rich lands and natural resources they once did.

Migration and Expansion

Colonization by Spain continued into the 1700s. Families from the northern Basque region of Spain arrived, bringing their unique language and culture. They valued hard work and business skills—important in building a thriving economy. These allowed them to build wealth and rise among the Spanish aristocracy in Chile. Today many of these rich and influential families still control much of the country's wealth and power.

European Immigrants

After Chile gained its independence from Spain in 1810, the new government created policies to encourage immigration from Europe to further develop the country's economy. English, French, and Italian **merchants** came to establish businesses in Chile's cities. German, Swiss, and Belgian immigrants established rural estancias—or farming estates—on Chile's southern grasslands. The country's grain and forestry industries began to grow significantly.

Spanish colonizers also brought their style of architecture to Chile, seen here on this building in Santiago.

The first German immigrants in Chile built homes with high-pitched roofs and wood shingles on the walls.

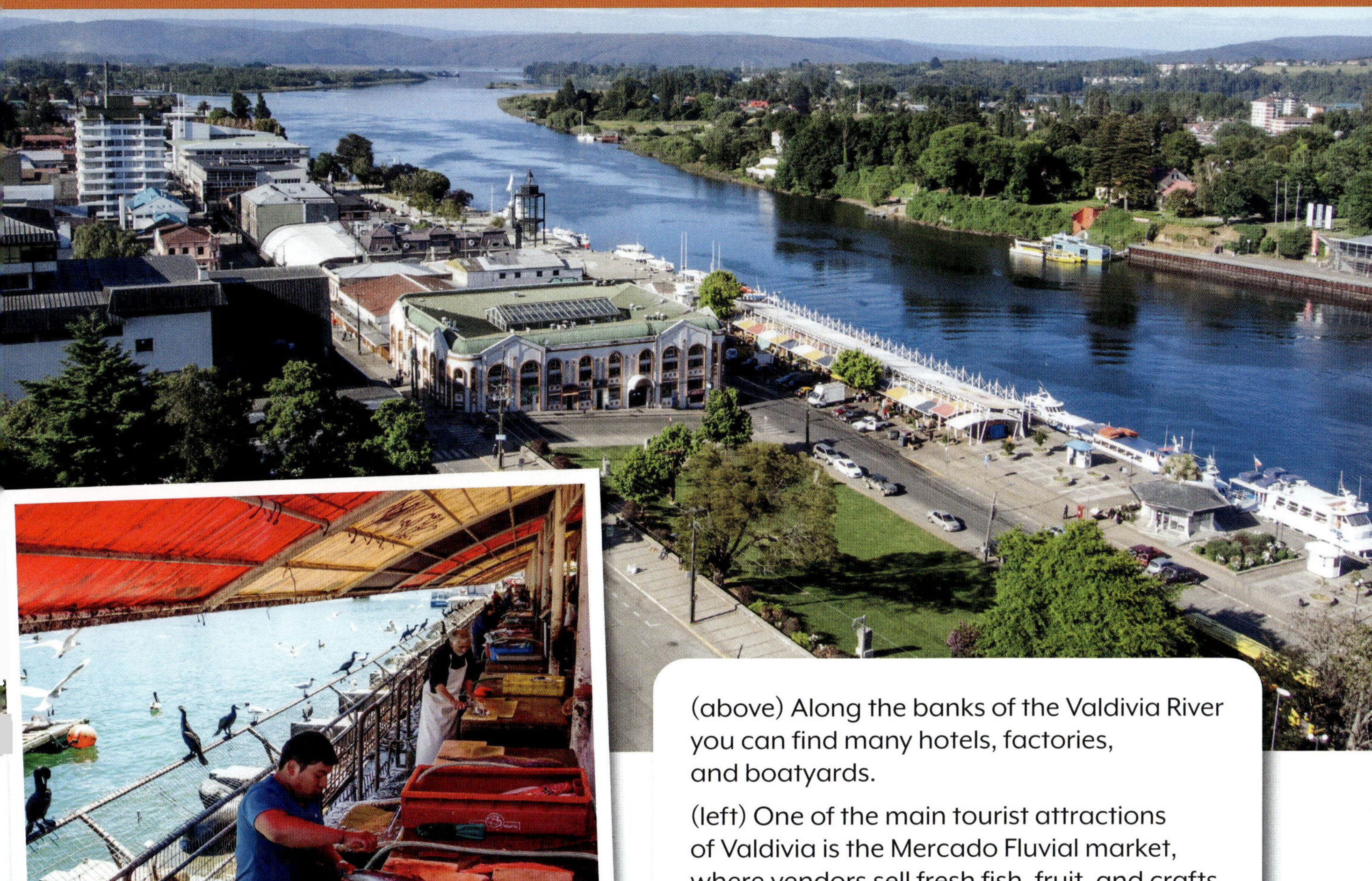

(above) Along the banks of the Valdivia River you can find many hotels, factories, and boatyards.

(left) One of the main tourist attractions of Valdivia is the Mercado Fluvial market, where vendors sell fresh fish, fruit, and crafts.

Important Cities

Chile's cities expanded and thrived with the arrival of immigrants from Europe. German settlers brought new skills that allowed cities to prosper. Valdivia—a strategically important city since its creation in 1552—became a strong manufacturing hub. Temuco had long been home to the Araucanian peoples. In 1881, it was established as a frontier outpost and soon became an important center for agriculture, livestock, and forestry. Santiago, founded by the Spanish in 1541, became the country's political, financial, and economic capital.

Restricting Indigenous Rights

As European settlers increased their power and influence across the country, the Chilean government began a policy to "Chileanize" their Indigenous peoples—to create one Chilean identity that would represent all ethnic groups. It believed this policy would help strengthen unity between Indigenous and non-Indigenous peoples. But it allowed the government to restrict Indigenous rights to land, culture, and identity. Instead of unity, it has led to severe inequalities and conflict. Indigenous tribes, who once controlled large areas of productive, fertile land, have been forced into more remote, poorer regions of the country.

Settling a Difficult Landscape

Chile's imposing mountain ranges, long ocean coastline, parched desert, and deep **fjords** have created significant challenges to human migration and how people have settled the country. At more than 2,600 miles (4,180 km) in length, it is the longest country in the world. Connecting people and economic activities from north to south is no easy task.

Working on the Railroad

Construction of a railway began in 1840. When complete, it spanned 1,900 miles (3,050 km)—from Arica in the north to Puerto Montt in the south. But maintaining the railway over these huge distances was challenging. Maintenance was expensive and travel times could be very long. As passenger and freight traffic declined, the railroad fell into disrepair. In the 1990s, the government committed to improving rail transportation between key cities. The most important link today is between Santiago and Valparaiso, Chile's largest urban centers.

The TerraSur is an express train that takes passengers from Santiago to Chillán in the south.

Connecting the Americas

The Pan-American Highway was first proposed in 1923 as a road to link North and South America. This was important for Chile, which wanted to develop its resources and expand economic ties with the U.S. Today the highway is a key transportation route. In Chile, it runs from Arica to Puerto Montt. It connects many agricultural centers along the way—including Rancagua, Curicó, Talca, and Los Ángeles.

Coastal Ports

Ocean seaports were established along the coast by Spanish explorers. These ports were the most efficient way to transport goods to and from markets overseas. Concepción—founded in 1550—provides access for the Central Valley's agriculture and forestry products. Talcahuano was founded in 1544 to defend nearby Spanish settlements. It was once used by American whaling ships, which docked there for fresh water and food. Today it is a key manufacturing and fisheries center. Antofagasta was established as an important port for the export of Chile's silver and saltpeter. Valparaiso was an important stopover for ships traveling between the Atlantic and Pacific Oceans until the Panama Canal opened in 1914 and provided a more efficient shipping route. Today it is an important tourist destination.

The Pan-American Highway is known as Route 5 through the Atacama Desert.

Talcahuano is an important port city. Its main exports include lumber, fur, hides, wool, and coal.

CHAPTER 3 Life Today

Modern Industry

The ranches established across the Patagonian grasslands by Spanish settlers helped transform this area into one of the world's most important sheep-farming regions. These animals are well-adapted to Patagonia's harsh climate and landscape. Wool weaving originated with Indigenous peoples who raised alpaca for their wool. Merino sheep are prized for their high-quality, luxurious wool. Today Chile produces more than 20 million pounds (9 million kg) of wool each year.

Chile's Easter Island is found off the west coast in the South Pacific Ocean. It is famous for its nearly 900 stone statues, called *moai*, that can be seen throughout the island. Tourism is the main industry that drives the island's economy.

Lithium

Mining remains one of Chile's most important resources. Copper makes up more than 60 percent of Chile's mineral exports. But lithium—a key ingredient in electric car batteries—is fast becoming one of Chile's most important resources. The Salar de Atacama, the enormous salt flat in northern Chile, contains the world's largest deposit of lithium. As the electric car market expands rapidly, Chile could play an important role in this industry. And lithium could power Chile's economy.

The Salar de Atacama produces one-third of the world's lithium supply.

Great Grape Growers

Chile's coastal climate—tucked between the Pacific Ocean and Andes Mountains—provides an ideal environment for growing grapes. Grapevines brought by Spanish settlers thrive in an area more than 800 miles (1,287 km) long on Chile's central coast. Over the years, Chile has emerged as the top exporter of table grapes and wine. Other agricultural products include cherries, cranberries, hazelnuts, wheat, and beef.

Fishing Industry

Chile's long ocean coastline also means an abundant supply of a wide variety of fish and seafood. Indigenous peoples have fished for a living here for thousands of years. Large fish farms have multiplied in recent decades to meet a growing global demand. Many raise non-native species for overseas markets. Increasingly, they pose a significant threat to the environment, native species, and local Indigenous fishing communities.

Tourism

Tourism has also developed as an important industry in Chile. Its dramatic and diverse landscapes provide an amazing variety of sights and activities to explore—from hiking, skiing, and surfing to wineries and Indigenous cultural experiences.

Torres del Paine National Park is a popular hiking destination that includes mountains, lakes, rivers, glaciers, and grasslands.

With more than 1,700 vineyards, the Colchagua Valley in Chile's Central Valley is one of South America's top wine-producing regions.

Life in the 21st Century

People in Chile today enjoy a lifestyle that is fairly **prosperous** and secure compared to many other countries in Latin America. Chile has a democratic government, which provides a relatively high degree of freedom for much of the urban population. But modern life in Chile still presents many challenges for Chile's Indigenous peoples.

Early Indigenous farmers and European settlers established rural settlements around farming, agriculture, and livestock. But most Chileans have migrated to urban centers in search of housing, education, jobs, and health care. In fact, Chile has a much higher urban population than many of its South American neighbors. Only about 1 in 10 Chileans live in rural settings today.

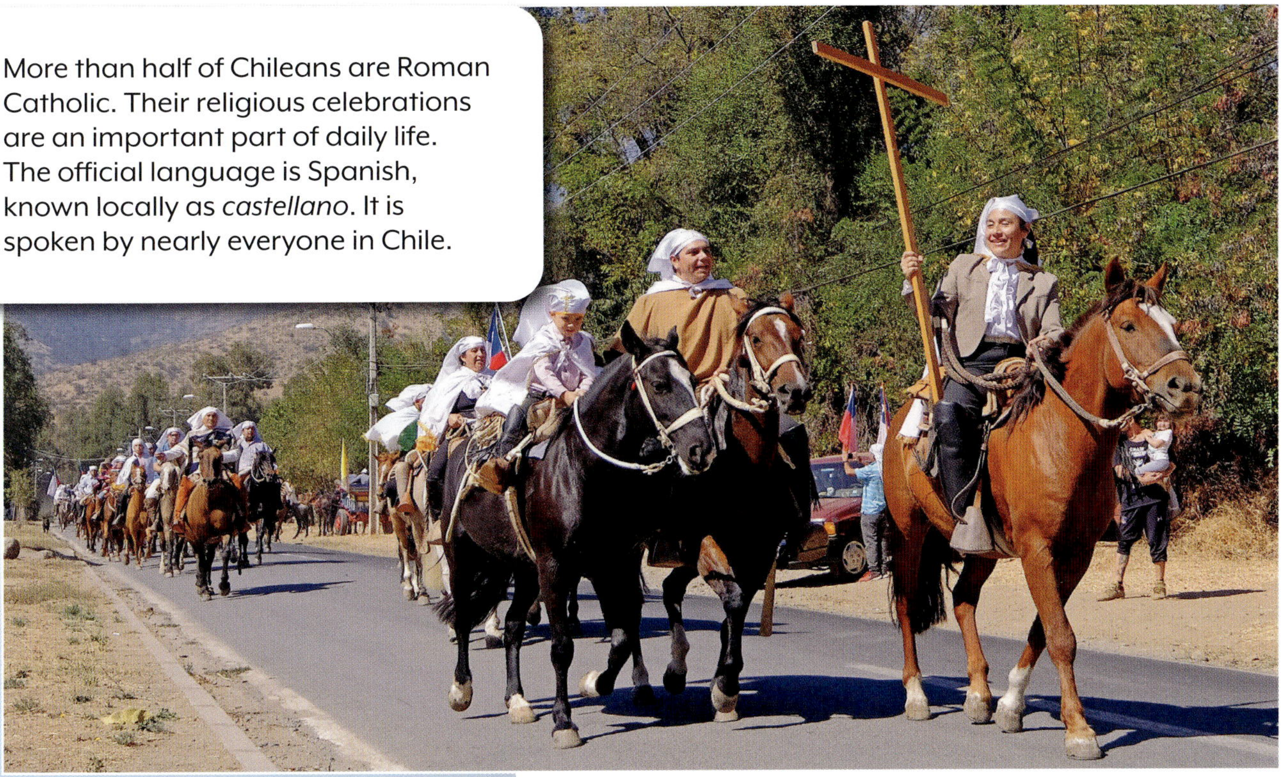

More than half of Chileans are Roman Catholic. Their religious celebrations are an important part of daily life. The official language is Spanish, known locally as *castellano*. It is spoken by nearly everyone in Chile.

Bicentennial Park in Santiago was named in celebration of Chile's 200th anniversary of independence.

Chile's Capital City

Almost half of Chile's population lives in or around the capital city, Santiago. It is the center of Chile's economy, and communications and transportation systems. It is a bustling city whose culture has been shaped by European and North American immigrants and cultures. Its wealthy, modern center—nicknamed "Sanhattan" after New York's Manhattan—contrasts sharply with the overcrowded, poor **slums** of the city's outer districts. Many Indigenous peoples have been forced to relocate to Santiago in search of jobs to support their families.

Cities often force the integration of rural and Indigenous populations, with little regard for their culture and traditions. A social-housing project in Santiago is one initiative that attempts to address this. The Ruca Dwellings Project provides traditional dwellings for Mapuche residents. It allows them to participate in modern society without giving up their traditional way of life. But there is much more work to do to help Indigenous peoples thrive in modern Chile.

Human Impact on Environment

Chile's rich natural resources have provided its people with unique opportunities to settle, develop, and prosper off the land. But this comes with challenges as well. Weak government regulations have allowed industries to **exploit** the environment with few consequences. For Indigenous peoples the results have been disastrous.

Large agricultural plantations in Chile's Central Valley have strained local water supplies in an area already under stress from expanding human settlement and **climate change**. A decade-long drought has seen lakes dry up and fertile land become cracked and **barren**. Large tracts of old-growth forest have been destroyed to create more agricultural land. Others have been cleared to plant exotic tree plantations, harvested for their wood. As these forests disappear, native wildlife habitats are threatened, and soil **erosion** has worsened.

Expanding Ranches

Patagonian grasslands once hosted large populations of wildlife, such as llama and huemel, a deer native to Chile. For thousands of years, Indigenous peoples made their living by farming and hunting there. Many were displaced by European settlers who were granted land by the government to establish agricultural and livestock ranches. As these ranches grew into larger **commercial** operations, more land has been cleared to accommodate them. This has transformed the landscape of the Chilean steppe, destroying the lifestyles of Indigenous farmers and herders.

Indigenous communities protest the mining of lithium on their land.

Salmon and mackerel are farmed south of Castro in the Chilean fjords.

Currently there are more than 12,000 sheep ranches throughout the Patagonian grasslands.

Mining's Damaging Effects

Chile's mining activities require enormous amounts of water in a desert area where water is already scarce. This threatens local Indigenous populations. Large areas of the desert have also been **contaminated** by mining activity, which threatens local wildlife, particularly the Andean flamingos that live in the salt marshes of the Atacama Desert.

Fish Farms

Indigenous peoples have relied on small-scale fishing for food for centuries. But as Chile has expanded its fishing operations to supply the global market, industrial fish farms have expanded along its coastline. Overproduction of farmed salmon has caused pollution as artificial feed and fish waste contaminate the waters. This reduces oxygen levels and threatens local species, as well as the Indigenous peoples who rely on them for food.

The Aymara people in northern Chile have become some of the most skilled farmers in South America. The unique farming techniques they have developed have enabled them to survive in their harsh environment.

Challenges for Indigenous Peoples

There are more than 2 million Indigenous peoples in Chile today, representing about 13 percent of Chile's population. The loss of their lands has resulted in their displacement and marginalization in Chile. Driven from their lands by Spanish settlers, they were forced to relocate to remote areas where the climate and terrain were more difficult for farming, hunting, and fishing. As rights to mineral resources, land, water, and forests were granted to European settlers, local Indigenous tribes found themselves further sidelined from the country's economic activity.

Many government policies have forced Indigenous peoples to choose between integrating into modern society or enduring the difficult conditions of the remote, rural communities they have been forced into. As a result, Indigenous peoples have a higher poverty rate, lower levels of education and health care, and poorer housing and jobs than non-Indigenous peoples. Their traditional culture and language have been threatened as well.

Closer Look

Chilean Constitution and Recognition of Indigenous Peoples

Mestizo Chileans are proud of the brave and fierce Mapuche warriors from which they are descended. But too little has been done to ensure that Indigenous culture, language, and traditions can thrive in modern Chile.

Chile adopted its constitution in 1980 to recognize the rights of all Chilean people. But the constitution recognizes people only as Chilean—with no recognition of their ethnic background. This means Indigenous peoples are not officially recognized under Chilean law. Without recognition of their existence, there is no acknowledgment of their rights.

Since 1990, a number of reforms to address this have been proposed, but never passed into law. In 1993, the Indigenous Peoples Act established the right of Mapuche people to participate in society and resource development. But in reality, it has done little to improve their situation. Protests and conflicts have taken place between Indigenous peoples and local governments. In late 2019, it was approved that a Constitutional Convention committee will revise the 1980 constitution. The committee, made up of 155 members, includes 17 seats reserved for Indigenous peoples. The nation will vote as to whether they approve the new constitution in September 2022.

In October 2019, 1.2 million people marched in the streets of Santiago to protest against social inequality.

Mapuche people protest against the construction of an airport on their land.

A 26-foot-tall (7.9 m) monument created to honor the bravery of the Mapuche people stands in Santiago's main square.

CHAPTER 4 A Vibrant Country

Most of today's Chileans are mestizo—descended from a mixed heritage of native Indigenous peoples and Spanish settlers who came here centuries ago. Many bear the names of the mighty Indigenous leaders of Chile's past—like Lautaro, Lincoyan, and Tucapel.

A Unique Chilean Identity

Chile is a country with many diverse landscapes and a long history of unique ethnic groups, cultures, and traditions. You might expect the character of its people to represent the individual regions in which they live, as well as their distinct histories. But, in fact, Chile has preferred to promote a singular identity of its people as simply "Chilean"—regardless of their ethnic backgrounds.

As the country has developed and modernized, Indigenous culture and heritage have not been properly recognized and supported as an important part of Chilean life. Indigenous leaders are now demanding greater recognition of their contribution to Chile's unique heritage. Some Indigenous traditions and celebrations are being rediscovered as the country begins to acknowledge their value in modern society.

Closer Look

Lautaro

Lautaro was a young Mapuche leader and warrior. He was born in 1535 and was the son of a Mapuche chief. His name—*Lef-Traru*—comes from the Mapuche language and means "swift hawk." He was captured and enslaved when he was a boy by the Spanish conquistador Pedro de Valdivia. As a groomsman for Valdivia, he learned horsemanship and Spanish battle strategies. When he was 15, he escaped and fled south to join the Araucanians. He worked to unite the local tribes, sharing what he'd learned from the Spanish conquerors. The Mapuche gave him the title of *toqui* to reflect his position as someone chosen to lead his people during times of war. At 18, he led an Indigenous uprising against the Spanish near the town of Tucapel. He captured and executed Valdivia but was killed in the Battle of Mataquito in 1557. He was only 22. He is one of the most important characters in the epic Spanish poem *La Araucana*, which illustrates the heroism of the Araucanian leaders.

Family and Leisure Time

Family plays a central role in the life of every Chilean. Children keep close ties with their parents well into their adult lives. Weekends are a time for gathering with family and friends. Meals are an important time for families to eat, chat, and celebrate together. The pace of life is much slower than we are used to in North America. Leisure time is important to Chileans, who value evenings and weekends as time to relax, entertain, or pursue some of the many sports offered by Chile's landscapes—from surfing and hiking, to skiing and snowboarding.

El trompo (left) and *el emboque* (right) are fun, challenging toys for children.

Children play games like *el trompo* and *el emboque*. In *el trompo*, competitors try to spin a top as long as possible, while keeping it inside a circular space or by knocking out their competitors' tops. The goal of *el emboque* is to flick a small bell-shaped cap on to the wooden handle to which it is attached by a piece of string. Soccer—known locally as *futbol*—is played everywhere throughout the country.

Families often enjoy meals with children, parents, and grandparents.

During a summer festival in Pichilemu, cowboys compete in a traditional competition known as *Trilla a yegua suelta*.

Machis are known to beat a *cultrun*, or ceremonial drum, during a ritual or ceremony.

Chilean Cowboy

The cowboy is a popular figure in Chilean life. It is a tradition that began on Chile's livestock ranches. Cowboys—or *huasos*—are admired as loyal, chivalrous, honest, and hard-working. They take part in many of Chile's national celebrations. Their traditional costume includes wide pants, a short jacket covered by a brightly colored poncho—or *chamanto*—and a straw hat, known as a *chupalla*. For special occasions, stirrups, spurs, and a red waistband are added.

Mapuche Beliefs

Mapuche traditions and beliefs are an important part of life in rural Chile. Their deep respect for nature is reflected in traditional prayer meetings, known as *machitunes*, where they ask the gods for rain to support their crops. Traditional *lonkos* (or chiefs) and *machis* (medicine healers) play central roles as spiritual leaders. Women pass down their textile skills to their daughters, and their traditional blankets and rugs are highly prized. The Mapuches' strong sense of community has spread across all levels of Chilean life.

Festivals and Celebrations

Chile's numerous festivals are lively and colorful. They reflect the country's rich history, cultural heritage, and diverse landscapes. The festival calendar is marked by celebrations that honor both Spanish and Indigenous traditions and beliefs.

Of all Chile's festivals, *Fiestas Patrias* is the most important. It takes place on September 18 to mark Chile's independence from Spain, which took place in 1810. People decorate their houses with the country's flag. Streets and city parks burst with people celebrating. Large barbecues—or *parrilladas*—are organized and the smell of delicious grilled meat fills the air. People dress up in their traditional costumes to dance the *cueca*, Chile's national dance.

Fiesta de la Vendimia takes place from March through May as the grapes grown in central Chile are prepared for harvest. Towns across the region celebrate the first batch of harvested grapes with a religious blessing. Local grape queens are crowned and weighed on a scale with bottles of wine. Teams compete in grape-stomping contests to see who is the fastest to crush a barrel full of grapes into juice. And, of course, there are parties, parades, dancing, and music!

The *Cueca* is a dance that symbolizes the courting of a rooster and a chicken.

Meat skewers known as *anticuchos* are a popular food grilled during *Fiestas Patrias.* They usually include beef, sausage, onion, and peppers.

The *diablada*, or Dance of the Devils, is the most widely known and ancient dances of *La Tirana.*

Important Indigenous Traditions

We Tripantu translates as "return of the Sun." It marks the shortest day of the year in the southern hemisphere and is one of the most important dates for Indigenous peoples in Chile. On June 23, they wait for the rising of the Sun to celebrate the renewed life and rebirth of the new year ahead. Traditional songs and dances are performed to honor the spirits of their ancestors.

One of the most vibrant and exciting festivals is *Fiesta de La Tirana*. It blends Catholic and Indigenous beliefs to honor the Spanish Virgen del Carmen, protector of fishers and sailors. Performers in elaborate costumes and masks perform the *diablada*—a dance which represents the devil and other characters from ancient Indigenous legends. Churches hold religious ceremonies and locals set up street stalls to sell handicrafts and food.

Chilean Cuisine

Porotos granados is a national dish of Chile. This hearty stew combines traditionally Indigenous ingredients—like corns, beans, and squash—with others introduced by the Spanish—like onions and garlic. Chile's long ocean coastline offers an abundance of fish, which feature in local dishes. *Machas* (razor clams), *cochayuyo* (seaweed), and *erizos* (sea urchins) are just a few. Bite-sized pastries filled with meat, cheese, or shellfish—known as empanadas—are a staple food in Chile. *Buen provecho*! Good appetite!

Chileans enjoy four meals a day, starting with a light breakfast. It is followed by an elaborate lunch, which is the most important meal. *La once* or "Elevenses" is an afternoon snack, named after British morning tea-time at eleven o'clock. *Once* in Spanish means eleven. Dinner is late—around eight or nine o'clock in the evening, and is a small, simple meal.

(top) *Porotos granados*, or Chilean bean stew, is made with cranberry beans, squash, and corn.

(middle) *Paila marina*, or seafood stew, is often served during holidays and family gatherings.

(bottom left) Meat skewers are usually cooked over hot coals.

(bottom right) Some empanadas may contain olives, raisins, or hard-boiled eggs.

Cultural highlights

Chile's national dance, the *cueca*, is thought to have roots in Spanish, Indigenous, and African cultures. It mimics the courtship of a chicken and a rooster. Dancers wave white handkerchiefs as they clap, stomp their feet, and circle one another. The handkerchief represents the chicken's feathers or the rooster's comb. The music accompanying the dance is lively and fun.

Traditional *cueca* dance

Although soccer is played everywhere, the rodeo is Chile's national sport. The tradition started in the 1500s, when the first cowboys—or *huasos*—journeyed into the mountains to herd young calves for branding. Chilean rodeos are unlike rodeos in other countries, which involve numerous events. A Chilean rodeo features two *huasos* who must work together to pin a cow against an arena wall. They are awarded points for the number of moves needed, as well as how well the cow is pinned in place. If the cow escapes or moves in the wrong direction, points are deducted from the *huasos*' score.

Chilean rodeos are two-day events. The rodeo season usually lasts from September until April.

CHAPTER 5

Looking to the Future

Chile's 21st-Century Challenge: Water Scarcity

In a country rich with glaciers, fjords, mountain rivers, and a long ocean coastline, the availability of water would not seem to be a likely environmental issue. But Chile has a growing and urgent water crisis.

It has suffered a drought for more than a decade that now affects more than 75 percent of the country. Despite some of the most advanced environmental laws on the continent, experts believe that Chile could be among the world's most water-stressed countries by 2040. This will have terrible consequences for Chile's people, wildlife, crop production, and industry.

Causes of the Crisis

Climate change is one of the most important factors. Higher temperatures, reduced rainfalls, and shrinking glaciers have caused water levels in lakes and rivers to decline. Unlimited water grants provided by the government to the mining, agriculture, and forestry industries have drained Chile's water resources. Large commercial plantations, which grow non-native, water-intensive crops for export, have strained the Central Valley's water supply. Growing human populations have put further demands on Chile's once plentiful water resources.

Alfalfa is a crop grown in the Central Valley in Chile using circular irrigation. The main water source for the Central Valley is from the Maípo River Basin. The basin is expected to decrease 40 percent in the next 50 years.

Most of the groundwater in the Atacama Desert is fossil water, or water left over from its past. Mining is quickly using up this **nonrenewable** water source.

Over a few short years, Laguna de Aculeo, a shallow lake near Santiago, has disappeared.

Devastating Effects

Chileans are already feeling the effects of this crisis. More than 1 million people across the country no longer have access to safe, clean drinking water. Crop and livestock production have been devastated and many small farmers struggle to earn a living. Conflicts between Indigenous communities, farmers, and industry have worsened as the fight for water becomes more desperate.

Finding a Solution

A number of solutions are being explored. The government must improve water regulation to ensure a fair and **sustainable** water supply to farmers, industries, and communities. Shifts toward more sustainable practices in agriculture—like **regenerative farming**, less water-intensive crops, and better irrigation systems—will be necessary. Restoring native tree plantations and forests will help minimize soil erosion and better withstand drought. Creative ideas such as harvesting water from fog, which is plentiful along Chile's extensive coastline, are also being developed.

Harnessing the Landscape

Chile's rich natural resources drive its export economy. As the country looks to the future, it will need to find sustainable ways to harness these resources while facing important environmental challenges. It has pledged to be **carbon neutral** by 2050. With its plentiful resources in wind, solar, and geothermal energy, there are a number of possibilities to explore.

The 50 turbines of the El Arrayán wind farm conserve enough water to meet the needs of around 11,000 Chileans.

Energy from the Earth

Geothermal energy is generated by the tremendous forces held within Earth's crust. With 15 percent of the world's volcanoes, Chile has an enormous opportunity to tap into geothermal energy resources. Cerro Pabellón, located in the Atacama Desert, is the first geothermal power plant in South America. Opened in 2017, it has the potential to power more than 150,000 homes and reduce the country's carbon emissions.

A geothermal camp operates at the base of the San Pedro Volcano, one of the tallest active volcanoes in the world.

Power of the Sun

The Atacama Desert is also an important source of solar power. Cerro Dominador, based there, is Chile's largest solar power project. It hopes to produce 20 percent of Chile's electricity from clean energy by 2025. Its aim is to reduce carbon emissions by 640,000 tons (580,598 metric tons) per year.

Wind Farms

Chile's Pacific coastline offers huge potential for wind energy. Small wind farms already power a number of communities along the coast. The largest—El Arrayán—is located near Coquimbo, north of Santiago. It supplies enough energy to power 200,000 households.

Protecting Nature's Resources

Recently, Chile has begun to look at reforms to its constitution that could help address environmental and social inequality issues. Indigenous groups believe that to guarantee our future on a healthy planet we must recognize our human ties to nature and Mother Earth, or Pachamama. They support a more environmentally sustainable approach to mining, forestry, and agricultural practices. And they are fighting for more control over the country's natural resources. They want to ensure that these industries have Indigenous consent and cooperation for projects as they are developed.

The Cerro Dominador solar farm uses 392,000 solar panels to collect the Sun's energy.

Protecting Indigenous Rights and Lands

Indigenous tribes in Chile once lived off the land and sea as hunters, farmers, and fishers. Today, almost 90 percent have become city-dwellers. Many have been forced off their lands—first by Spanish colonizers, and later by industry and government-supported businesses. Few have received any of the wealth from the families and organizations that control these industries.

The Wiphala is a colorful square emblem often used as a flag to represent the Aymara people.

In 2007, Chile adopted the UN Declaration on the Rights of Indigenous Peoples. But the Indigenous peoples' fight for recognition of their lands, culture, and traditions has still not been won. They continue to face threats and violence from government-supported industries that try to silence their voices and ignore their demands for equal rights. With the rewriting of the constitution, Indigenous leaders hope this will provide them with an opportunity to play a greater role in society in order to ensure their equality as citizens of Chile.

In the ancient Pachamama ceremony, nothern Indigenous people give an offering to Mother Earth, and say a prayer or request for the future.

Closer Look

Alberto Curamil

Mapuche communities have increasingly protested against government discrimination and demanded the return of their ancestral lands in recent years. For doing this, many Indigenous activists have been labeled as terrorists and criminals. No one knows this better than Alberto Curamil. Curamil is an outspoken Mapuche tribesman from central Chile's Araucanía region. Like many Indigenous leaders, he has faced threats, fines, arrest, and imprisonment for doing so. When Chile announced a huge hydroelectric project on Araucanía's rivers in 2010 during the worst drought in Chile's history, Curamil began to organize his people. He led protests, marches, and blockades, gathered advice from environmental experts, and launched a legal challenge against the government. Six years after the project was first announced, the government canceled it. Curamil's successful campaign saved an important ecosystem from further destruction and worsening drought conditions.

Curamil has dedicated his life to protecting the region's lands, forests, and rivers, as well as Mapuche traditions and language.

Curamil's work on the hydroelectric campaign gained him a prestigious Goldman Environmental Prize, nicknamed the "green Nobel Prize."

adobe A type of clay that is molded into bricks and used for buildings

anticyclone A system of rotating winds around a center of high pressure that pushes apart and sinks; opposite to a cyclone

arable Suitable for growing crops

arid Too dry to support vegetation; having very little rainfall

barren Land on which very few plants grow

carbon neutral Referring to a state where the amount of carbon dioxide emitted is the same as what's absorbed

climate change The long-term changes of the world's temperature and weather patterns

coarse Rough or prickly

colonization The process by which a country takes control of another country or area by occupying it

commercial Concerned with buying and selling goods and services

conquistadors Spanish conquerors who set out to colonize what they called the "New World," or the Americas

constitution The basic laws and principles by which a country is governed

contaminated Made unclean, or polluted

displace To force people to leave the area where they live

domesticated Tame animals kept as pets or livestock

erosion Gradually wearing away

exploit To use something or someone unfairly for your own advantage

export To sell goods or services to another country

fault line A crack in Earth's crust along which earthquakes usually occur

fertile Able to produce crops

fertilizer A chemical or substance added to soil to make plants more fertile

fjord A long, narrow inlet with cliffs on either side

ghost town A town or city that has been abandoned with few or no inhabitants left

hardy Able to survive hard or difficult conditions

Incan civilization A large empire that lasted from the 1400s to early 1500s that inhabited the land along the Pacific Coast from Ecuador to the Maule River in Chile

Indigenous Native to a particular place. Indigenous peoples are the original inhabitants of a place.

inhospitable An environment that is difficult and hard to live in

irrigation The agricultural process of supplying water to crops

marginalized Treated as insignificant or unimportant

merchant Someone who buys and sells goods for profit

mestizo A person of mixed Spanish and Indigenous descent

native Originally from a particular place

nitrate A chemical compound containing nitrogen and oxygen molecules, often used in fertilizers

nomadic Moving from place to place

nonrenewable Not able to be renewed or replenished

oasis Water in a desert where vegetation grows

plantation A large farm or agricultural estate

plateaus Large areas of high, flat ground

prosperous Successful; having a lot of money

regenerative farming Farming practices that seek to conserve and enhance the well-being of the environment and surrounding ecosystem

reservation An area of land set aside by the government for Indigenous peoples

runoff The draining away of water

seaport A town or city with a harbor for seagoing ships

slum A very poor, overcrowded urban area

steppe A dry, flat grassland with no trees

subantarctic Relating to the area just north of the Antarctic Circle

sustainable Able to be used in a way that does not deplete natural resources or cause significant environmental damage

temperate Having temperatures that are not too hot and not too cold

terraces A series of flat areas cut out of a hill to plant crops or a garden

treaty A formal, written agreement between two parties

UNESCO World Heritage site A protected landmark or area singled out by the United Nations Educational, Scientific, and Cultural Organization as being globally significant

urbanization The process by which an area or country changes from mostly rural to more urban, with more cities

Books

Bowman, Chris. *Chile* (Country Profiles). Bellwether Media, 2020.

Burgan, Michael. *Chile* (Enchantment of the World). Children's Press, 2016.

Dobson-Largie, Claudia. *Country Jumper in Chile.* Independent Publisher, 2019.

Martin, Paula, and Margaret Read MacDonald. *Pachamama Tales: Folklore from Argentina, Bolivia, Chile, Paraguay, Peru, and Uruguay.* Libraries Unlimited, 2014.

Peppas, Lynn. *The Atacama Desert* (Deserts Around the World). Crabtree Publishing, 2013.

Websites

Fun facts about the country, its people, culture, history, and more:
https://kids.nationalgeographic.com/geography/countries/article/chile

A photo slideshow of Chile's most spectacular landscapes, with a description of each:
https://www.nationalgeographic.com/travel/slideshow/paid-content-experience-chiles-natural-playground

Learn more about Chile's food, culture, people, and geography:
https://www.kids-world-travel-guide.com/chile-facts.html

Detailed information about the country, its economy, government, land, and climate:
https://kids.britannica.com/students/article/Chile/273638

agriculture/farming 11, 14, 15, 17, 18, 19, 20, 21, 23, 24, 25, 26, 28, 40, 41, 43, 44
alpacas 4, 5, 10, 16, 24
Altiplano 4
Andes Mountains 4, 6, 8, 9, 10, 11, 25
Araucanians 17, 19, 21, 33, 45
Atacama Desert 9, 10, 11, 12, 13, 16, 23, 24, 29, 42, 43
Aymara 4, 5, 6, 16, 30, 44

celebrations 27, 32, 35, 36, 37
Central Valley 8, 14, 18, 19, 23, 28, 40
ceremonies 37
children 5, 17, 34
"Chileanize" 21
cities 6, 8, 20, 21, 22, 23, 27, 36, 44
climate 4, 6, 9, 10, 14, 15, 18, 24, 25, 28, 30
climate change 28, 40
colonization 6, 14, 15, 19, 20
conquistadors 18, 33
constitution 6, 31, 43, 44
copper 9, 12, 24
costumes 5, 35, 36, 37
cowboys 35, 39
crops 4, 5, 8, 11, 13, 14, 16, 17, 18, 35, 40, 41
culture 6, 16, 17, 20, 21, 27, 30, 31, 32, 39, 44
Curamil, Alberto 45

dancing 5, 36, 37, 39
democracy 26

earthquakes 6
education 26, 30
European settlers 14, 21, 24, 25, 26, 28, 30, 32
exports 8, 10, 12, 15, 23, 24, 25, 40, 42

family 5, 14, 17, 20, 27, 34, 44
fertilizers 13
festivals 36, 37
fishing 10, 15, 17, 19, 23, 25, 29, 30, 37, 44
fjords 22, 29, 40
food 4, 13, 15, 17, 23, 29, 36, 37, 38
forests/forestry 11, 15, 20, 21, 23, 28, 30, 40, 41, 43, 45

games 34
geothermal 42
glaciers 40
government 19, 20, 21, 22, 26, 28, 30, 31, 40, 41, 44, 45
grapes 14, 25, 36

health care 26, 30
homes 4, 5, 21, 42

Incan civilization 12, 18
Indigenous peoples 6, 10, 14, 15, 16, 17, 18, 19, 21, 24, 25, 26, 27, 28, 30, 31, 32, 33, 36, 37, 38, 39, 40, 43, 44, 45
industry 10, 11, 13, 20, 24, 25, 28, 40, 41, 43, 44
immigrants 20, 21, 27
irrigation 8, 40, 41

Lautaro 32, 33
lithium 9, 24, 28
llamas 4, 5, 10, 16, 17, 28

Mapuche 6, 11, 17, 18, 19, 27, 31, 33, 35, 45
mestizo 6, 31, 32
mining 12, 13, 24, 28, 29, 40, 43
music 5, 36, 39, 44

natural resources 6, 19, 28, 42, 43

Pan-American highway 23
Patagonian 14, 17, 24, 28
plantations 11, 15, 28, 40, 41
pollution 29
potatoes 4, 14, 17

railroad 22
ranches 10, 14, 24, 28, 29, 35
religion 27, 37
rivers 8, 18, 21, 40, 45
rodeos 39

Santiago 6, 7, 8, 20, 21, 22, 27, 31, 41, 43, 44
salt 4, 10, 11, 24, 29
seaports 8, 23
sheep 4, 14, 24, 28, 29
solar energy 42, 43
Spanish 6, 14, 18, 19, 20, 21, 23, 25, 27, 30, 33, 36, 37, 38, 39, 44
sports 34, 39
steppes 4, 10, 11, 14, 28
subantarctic 9, 10, 15

tourism 13, 23, 24, 25
traditions 4, 5, 27, 30, 31, 32, 35, 36, 37, 39, 44, 45
tsunamis 6

urbanization 11, 22, 26

Valparaiso 8, 22, 23
villages 4, 19

water 9, 15, 17, 23, 28, 29, 30, 40, 41, 42
weaving 5, 10, 24
wildlife 10, 28, 29, 40
wind 9, 42, 43
wool 5, 10, 14, 17, 18, 24

About the Author

Linda Barghoorn has written thirty children's books for which she studied a wide range of topics, from deserts and earthquakes to refugees, resilient cities, and remarkable people. She is an avid learner, explorer, and traveler. When she's not at work, she can most often be found hiking or curled up with a good book.